POKÉMON ™

MY POKÉMON ADVENTURE JOURNAL

GOTTA CATCH 'EM ALL!™

Pokémon come in all shapes and sizes – they're unique, just like you! Each individual Pokémon has its own personality – there are a lot of Pikachu, but no two are the same!

Inside this book, you'll discover lots of amazing secrets about Pokémon and reveal some exciting new things about you, too.

Get ready – your adventure is about to begin!

ALL ABOUT YOU

Every amazing adventure starts with a hero and that hero is you! This is your journal, so use the space below to fill in all about you and your favourite things.

Name: _____

Nickname: _____

Age: _____ Date of birth: _____

Draw a picture or stick a photo of yourself here.

There are hundreds of Pokémon and tons of exciting things to discover, but we all have our favourites – what are yours?

Types of Pokémon: _____

_____

_____

Pokémon region: _____

Pokémon Trainers: _____

_____

_____

_____

_____

Pokémon gym: _____

_____

AMAZING ADVENTURES

There's so much to discover and always plenty of Pokémon to catch. Make a note of all the amazing things you're yet to do.

Top five Pokémon I'd love to catch:

1. _____

2. _____

3. _____

4. _____

5. _____

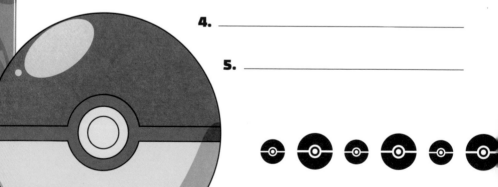

Which region would you most like to explore?

_____

Why? _____

_____

Is there a gym badge you haven't won?

_____

What can you do to help you win this badge?

_____

_____

_____

_____

ALL ABOUT YOUR LIFE

After a busy day battling, Trainers can rest and recharge their Pokémon at the Pokémon Centre. Remember, it's important for you to have some downtime, too.

Draw a picture or stick a photo of your bedroom here.

Your favourite thing about your bedroom is:

Your favourite things to do in your room:

_____

_____

_____

Sleep like a
Snorlax?

Dance like
Ludicolo?

You and your Pokémon are like one big happy family.
Write about all the other special people in your life.

Describe your family: _____

_____

Draw a picture or stick a photo of your family here.

POKÉMON PALS

Ash has met lots of amazing people on his adventures, and his best friend is his Pokémon Pikachu. Having a close group of friends is heaps of fun. Write about yours here!

Who are your best friends?

_____

_____

How did you all meet? _____

_____

What makes your friendship so special? Do you like to train together? Or maybe you have the same favourite Pokémon?

_____

_____

One of the greatest things about friendship is sharing —
whether it's Poké Balls or secrets. Share this book with
your friends by asking them to fill in all about
their favourite Pokémon.

Name: _____

Favourite Pokémon:

_____

Because: _____

_____

**List three things that
make you a top Trainer:**

1. _____

2. _____

3. _____

Name: _____

Favourite Pokémon:

_____

Because: _____

_____

**List three things that
make you a top Trainer:**

1. _____

2. _____

3. _____

BE A POKÉMON

**If you could be a Pokémon, what would you be?
Would you have a flaming tail like Charizard
or a beautiful voice like Jigglypuff?**

My Pokémon name: _____

My Pokémon type: _____

My region: _____

My strengths:

1. _____

2. _____

3. _____

My best moves:

1. _____

2. _____

3. _____

Draw yourself as a Pokémon here:

STUDY TIME

When you're not busy training with your Pokémon, it's important to study hard and keep your mind active.

What is your favourite thing about school?

_____

Which are your favourite subjects? Why?

_____

_____

Do you have any hobbies or activities that you enjoy outside of school?

_____

_____

Design your own Pokémon academy where Trainers can hone their skills and learn more about all the amazing Pokémon.

The name of your Pokémon academy:

_____

What classes would you take? Describe them below.

_____

_____

Draw your Pokémon academy here!

GREAT GAMES

Pikachu has put together these games that are perfect
for playing with your pals.

Which Pokémon?

Am I a Water-type
Pokémon?

Do I have wings?

Write the name of one of your favourite
Pokémon on a sticky note and ask your friends
to do the same. Then all swap notes (without looking)
and stick the one you get to your forehead.

Take turns asking each other "yes or no" questions
to try to guess your Pokémon. Whoever gets theirs right
in the least number of questions is the winner!

Is one of my
moves Thunder
Shock?

Pokémon Pairs

Cover all the Pokémon below with small pieces of paper and, playing with a friend,
take turns removing one piece from each Pokémon. If the Pokémon match,
keep the paper and give yourself a point. If they don't, replace the paper
and keep playing until all the pairs have been found!

Poké Balls and Crosses

Playing with a friend, take turns drawing your symbol (a round ball or a cross) in the grid. The first to get three in a row horizontally, vertically or diagonally wins!

POKÉMON TRAINER PROFILE

Ash dreams of becoming a Pokémon Master.
In order to achieve this, he trains hard and learns
everything he can about Pokémon. Do you dream
of being a top Trainer just like Ash?

Draw yourself as a Trainer with
your Pokémon by your side.

**What type of
Pokémon would
you specialise in?**

What do you think you need to do to be the very best Trainer you can be?

_____

_____

You're about to start your Pokémon quest! What would you bring with you on your journey? Don't forget to pack your Poké Balls!

_____

_____

_____

_____

_____

_____

MY POKÉMON TEAM

Who is in your Pokémon team?
Draw pictures of your Pokémon in their Poké Balls.
Write your favourite thing about each Pokémon underneath.

Pokémon name: _____

Pokémon name: _____

_____

_____

Pokémon name:

_____

Pokémon name:

_____

_____

_____

_____

_____

Pokémon name:

_____

Pokémon name:

_____

_____

_____

REAL REWARDS

Setting yourself goals and challenges will help you become a better Trainer, and it can be fun if you award yourself points for doing good things. Each deed scores points that could add up to treats, or even some extra time to spend on adventures with your Pokémon.

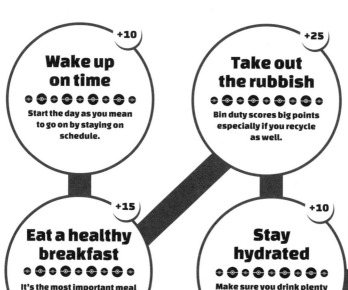

+10

Wake up on time

Start the day as you mean to go on by staying on schedule.

+25

Take out the rubbish

Bin duty scores big points especially if you recycle as well.

+15

Eat a healthy breakfast

It's the most important meal of the day and fuel for your body and brain.

+10

Stay hydrated

Make sure you drink plenty of water. It's healthier than sugary drinks.

Make a cup of tea +10

Adults love tea. Just be careful with the hot water.

Phone your relatives +15

It's good to talk to someone who hasn't heard from you in a while.

Eat your 5-a-day +30

Fruit and vegetables are good for you and can make you more alert.

REWARD

You got 100 points! You win 15 minutes of time with your Pokémon.

Tidy your room +10

Probably a good idea to do this on bin night. Don't forget under the bed.

Pay someone a compliment +15

It is important to make people feel acknowledged and loved.

Brush your teeth +15

– until they're gleaming. And don't forget to floss.

REWARD

You got over 50 points! Give yourself a treat for all your great work.

Train with your Pokémon +20

So that they're ready to battle.

POKÉMON PARTNERS

Ash and Pikachu are best friends, they'll always be there for each other. Whether you and your Pokémon are perfect partners or see things differently, you can find your friendship score using this calculation.

1. First, write **"THE POWER OF FRIENDSHIP"** on a piece of paper.

2. Then write your name underneath, and count how many times each letter of your name appears in "THE POWER OF FRIENDSHIP". Make sure you record the number under each letter.

3. Add up the numbers underneath your name. If you get a double figure, add those two numbers together so you're left with a single number (for example, 15 would become 6).

4. Now choose your favourite Pokémon, and repeat these steps with their name.

5. To find your friendship score, put the two numbers next to each other – so if your number is 4 and your Pokémon's is 7, you have a friendship score of 47%.

Here's an example to help you:

Ash Ketchum
012030200 = 8

Pikachu
2100020 = 4

THE POWER OF FRIENDSHIP
Friendship score: 84%

Your score...

Friendship score: 0–25%
You still have lots to learn about each other, but you can become even closer by spending more quality time together.

Friendship score: 26–50%
You're already a great team, but you don't always agree on everything. Make sure you always listen to each other and you'll be able to face anything together.

Friendship score: 51–75%
You and your Pokémon love to share – whether it's jokes or secrets. Even though you know each other so well already, there is still lots more to discover.

Friendship score: 76–100%
You two were meant to be, and a friendship like yours is truly special! You know you can always rely on each other.

ON THE TRAIL

You'll come across lots of Pokémon on your adventures, some more difficult to catch than others. As a Trainer, you'll learn new skills with each catch!

What do you think are the top skills needed for catching Pokémon?

_____

_____

_____

_____

_____

_____

Throwing an excellent curveball!

Using the right type of Pokémon in battle.

The first Pokémon I caught was:

_____

How I felt when I caught my first Pokémon:

_____

MVP! The Most Valuable Pokémon I've caught:

_____

The rarest Pokémon I've caught:

_____

Legendary Pokémon I've caught:

_____

Time to flee! The Pokémon I wish I'd caught but it ran away:

_____

POKÉ BALL POWER

There are lots of different Pokémon and different Poké Balls to help you catch them all. You won't get far without a pocketful of these.

Great Ball
A high-performance Poké Ball that provides a higher success rate for catching Pokémon than a standard Poké Ball.

Ultra Ball
An ultra-high-performance Poké Ball that provides a higher success rate for catching Pokémon than a Great Ball.

Master Ball
A rare Poké Ball that can capture any Pokémon without fail.

What would your dream Poké Ball look like? Draw it below and then write about what it can do.

_____

_____

_____

BIG BATTLES

Battles help Trainers to test the skills of their Pokémon. Write about some of your most memorable battles here.

Me vs Pokémon involved:

_____

Moves used:

_____

Coolest moments:

_____

What I learned from the battle:

_____

_____

Draw a picture of your best Pokémon battle.

YOUR PATH

It's important to stay true to yourself. Take this quiz to discover the special strength that makes you a top Trainer.

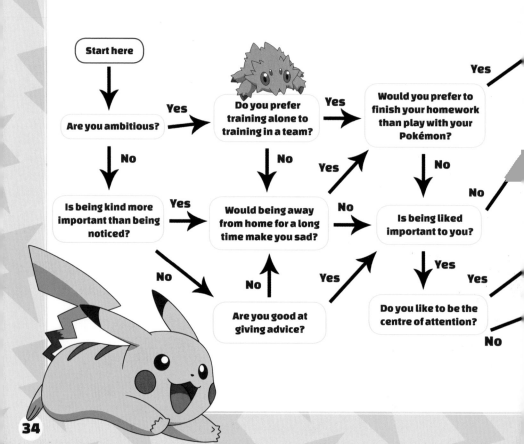

Start here

Are you ambitious? — **Yes** → Do you prefer training alone to training in a team? — **Yes** → Would you prefer to finish your homework than play with your Pokémon? — **Yes**

Are you ambitious? — **No** → Is being kind more important than being noticed?

Do you prefer training alone to training in a team? — **No** → Would being away from home for a long time make you sad?

Is being kind more important than being noticed? — **Yes** → Would being away from home for a long time make you sad?

Is being kind more important than being noticed? — **No** → Are you good at giving advice?

Would being away from home for a long time make you sad? — **Yes** →

Would being away from home for a long time make you sad? — **No** → Is being liked important to you?

Would you prefer to finish your homework than play with your Pokémon? — **No** → Is being liked important to you?

Are you good at giving advice? — **No** →

Are you good at giving advice? — **Yes** →

Is being liked important to you? — **Yes** → Do you like to be the centre of attention?

Do you like to be the centre of attention? — **Yes**

Do you like to be the centre of attention? — **No**

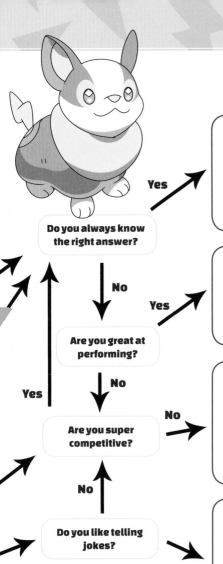

Do you always know the right answer?

Yes →

Smart 🔴
Everyone comes to you for the great advice you give. You're bright, thoughtful and considerate. You're often busy learning everything you can about Pokémon, but you always make time for your friends.

No ↓

Are you great at performing?

Yes →

Confident 🔴
You like to take the lead, and people look up to you. You're happy to make the difficult decisions, but you always make sure you consider other people's opinions.

No ↓

Are you super competitive?

No →

Thoughtful 🔴
You're kind, caring and a great listener. Friends and family are close to your heart, and you always make time for the Pokémon and people in your life. Your endless loyalty means you're good at keeping secrets and trustworthy to the end.

No ↑

Do you like telling jokes?

Yes →

Positive 🔴
You always look on the bright side of life! You can make your friends laugh, even when they're sad. Your cheerful and upbeat attitude means that you never give up, even when the going gets tough.

Yes ↑

MAKE YOUR MOVE

Your Pokémon train hard to be the best they can in battle and it's important for you to do the same.

Get active with this fun game and practise amazing moves just like your favourite Pokémon.

1. Ask an adult to help you cut out the action cards on the next page.

2. Jumble the action cards up and put them in a bowl or a jar.

3. Close your eyes and pick out an action card, and say "Pokémon Trainer (insert your name) says," and perform the action.

Hydro Pump like Blastoise.

Do an Air Slash like Pidgey.

Perform a Thunderbolt like Pikachu.

X-Scissor like Sandshrew.

Do a Tail Whip like Nidoqueen.

Do a Fire Spin like Vulpix.

Fury Swipes like Meowth.

Do a Dual Chop like Machop.

Stomp like Ponyta.

Yawn like Slowpoke.

Roar like Aerodactyl.

Bounce like Spoink.

Lick like Lickitung.

Howl like Loudred.

Tickle like Aipom.

Snore like Snorlax.

BATTLE READY

Which three moves do you think are the coolest?

1. _____

2. _____

3. _____

Come up with your own amazing moves!

Name of move: _____

What would your move do? _____

_____

_____

_____

TIME TO TRAIN

If you want to be the best, like no one ever was, you're going to have to take down Gym Leaders along the way.

The hardest Gym Leader I've fought is:

_____

The easiest Gym Leader I've fought is:

_____

Gym Badges I've earned:

_____

_____

What would your Pokémon Gym be called?

_____

What would your gym specialise in? (Pokémon type)

_____

How would you describe the gym structure?
(For example, Pewter City's Gym has boulders.)

_____

What would the badge you give out be called?

_____

Design your Gym Badge here and cut it out ready
to award to any hopeful Trainers.

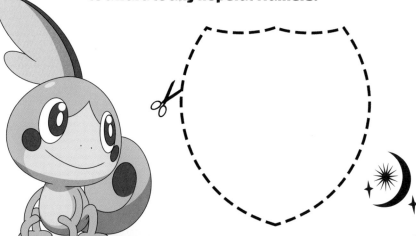

**What would your victory phrase be? (A speech if you win –
for instance, "Better luck next time, kid.")**

_____

**What would your defeat phrase be? (A speech if you lose –
such as, "Well done, the badge is yours!")**

_____

**What would be your opening phrase? (When you welcome a
Trainer to your Gym – for example, "So, have you got what it
takes?")**

_____

Ready to battle? Draw a picture of your Pokémon Gym.

ROLE MODEL

A role model is someone who sets a good example for you to follow. A top Trainer like Ash Ketchum can be a great role model to have ... but maybe you have someone else in mind! Write about a special person you admire and respect.

The name of my role model is:

_____

I admire them because:

_____

Three strengths they have that I admire are:

1. _____

2. _____

3. _____

Draw or stick a picture of your role model here.

Your role model can be real or from a story, a family member, a Trainer or even your favourite Pokémon, like Pikachu!

POKÉMON POWER

Need a boost? A happiness jar is a way to store good thoughts. Make your own and pick out a special note each day when you are feeling down, facing a challenge or just want to smile!

1. Choose a jar that's large enough to hold your happiness notes.

2. Ask an adult to help you carefully cut out the notes on the opposite page.

3. Fold the notes and pop them in the jar.

4. Add more notes over time – why not write down things that make you happy?

5. Take a note from the jar to read whenever you need a little Pokémon power in your life!

Channel your inner Charizard!

You are a bright spark!

 Never stop singing!

Be the very best!

Believe in Mew!

DISCOVER MORE

There are hundreds of Pokémon with amazing talents and skills, but it's important to remember that there are lots of special things about you that make you awesome, too.

It's time to discover more about your abilities and complete fun activities alongside some of your favourite Pokémon. Reveal your strengths and weaknesses with Onix, train hard with Machamp, plan a Pokémon party with Pikachu and much more!

BE STRONG

On your adventures, you're bound to come across a lot of
Normal-type Pokémon. Even though they're more common,
these Pokémon are all unique, just like you. Write about some
of the things that make you awesome.

People often compliment you on:

_____

You give really good advice about:

_____

A time when someone said they were proud of you:

_____

A time when you were proud of yourself:

_____

People always go to you for help with:

Do you have a hidden talent?

BUILD ON UP

Just like Pokémon, everyone has their strengths and weaknesses – write about yours here!

Three strengths you have are:

1. _____

2. _____

3. _____

Nobody is perfect! Three weaknesses you have are:

1. _____

2. _____

3. _____

What can you do to help turn these weaknesses into strengths?

_____

Which Pokémon do you think is the strongest? Why?

_____

_____

Which Pokémon do you think is the weakest? Why?

_____

_____

_____

_____

BE BRAVE

Steel-type Pokémon like Steelix might seem tough from the outside, but even the strongest Pokémon need help to feel brave. Never be afraid to ask for help when you need it, and remember, you're stronger than you think!

Write about a time you did something you were afraid to try. How did you feel afterwards?

_____

_____

What would you tell a Pokémon who was afraid to try a new move?

_____

What would you tell a friend who was anxious before a Pokémon battle?

_____

What is the bravest thing you've ever done? How did it make you feel?

_____

_____

What is the bravest thing your Pokémon has ever done? How did it make you feel to watch your Pokémon be brave?

_____

_____

_____

_____

_____

_____

_____

FAR TO FLY

From Kanto to Galar, there are so many amazing regions to explore! Take your Pokémon on an exciting journey and make new memories together.

If you could go to any Pokémon region, where would you go?

_____

Where would you stay?

_____

Who would you go with?

_____

What would you do?

_____

Which Pokémon would you want to catch?

_____

Making Memories

Keeping special souvenirs, like photos and tickets, can help you remember the adventures you have with your friends. Stick some of your keepsakes below.

DARE TO DREAM

Dragon-type Pokémon are mysterious creatures, and many can fly off to distant regions. Even if you don't go far, adventures make awesome stories. Use this story planner to help you write your own amazing Pokémon adventure!

The Start

Answer these questions to set the scene.

What's the weather like? _____

What can you see and hear? _____

Who is with you? They will be your main characters.

_____

_____

Will your story have magic in it?   Yes   No

The Middle
This is where the main excitement will happen!

Think of something that suddenly goes wrong or stops your journey.

_____

How do you and your main characters react?

_____

Do you have a plan?

_____

The End
Your story will finish as the journey comes to an end.

Describe how the problem was resolved: _____

_____

Is the journey finished? _____

What happens when you arrive at your destination?

_____

GO GREEN

Grass-type Pokémon can often be found soaking up the sun in the great outdoors. Take this book outside with you and go exploring. Write about what you discovered on your adventure here.

_____

_____

_____

_____

_____

_____

_____

LET IT GROW

Each time you have a creative thought write or draw it here.
Use this page to plant the seed and watch your ideas grow.

KEEP IT COOL

The skills and tactics you learn as a Trainer can help you in your everyday life.

List three problems or challenges that you're facing right now. How do you plan to tackle each of them?

Challenge: _____

Plan of action:

_____

_____

How my Pokémon can help me:

_____

_____

Challenge: _____

Plan of action:

_____

_____

How my Pokémon can help me:

_____

_____

Challenge: _____

Plan of action:

_____

_____

How my Pokémon can help me:

_____

_____

TRAIN HARD

As a Trainer, you'll need to keep your Pokémon strong and healthy, too. What do you do with your Pokémon to keep them fighting fit?

Every Pokémon enjoys something a little different to eat! Write down some of your Pokémon's favourite treats.

_____

_____

It's fun to cook up treats with your Pokémon, but don't forget about yourself. Write down three healthy foods that you like to eat:

1. _____

2. _____

3. _____

Write down three sports or exercises that you enjoy:

1. _____

2. _____

3. _____

Check out these tips to get active.

Throwing shapes!
Have someone in charge of the tunes while everyone else dances. When they press pause, the dancers all freeze, holding their pose for ten seconds. Play the game for ten minutes, striking a different pose each time!

Like a flash!
One person should grab a stopwatch, while the other does the workout. Run on the spot for 30 seconds, then throw in a move like a star jump. Repeat three times with a different move each time. Swap over, and see if your friend can follow your moves!

Stretch it out!
Find a space and stand up straight. Raise your arms and stretch up to the sky for ten seconds. Then bend down and touch your toes for ten seconds. Repeat three times.

RIDE A WAVE

Write down some of your best memories of hanging out with your friends, family and Pokémon. What made each moment special?

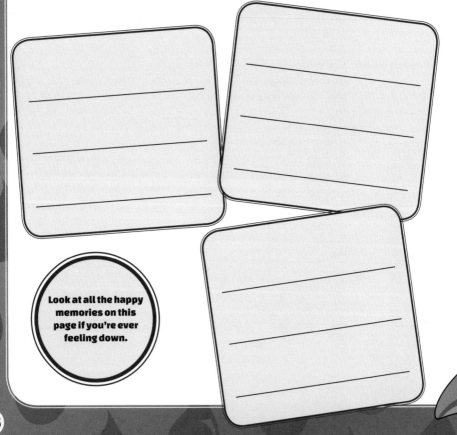

Look at all the happy memories on this page if you're ever feeling down.

FLAME ON

Even Pokémon have their good and bad days. If Charizard becomes angry, the flame at the tip of their tail can flare up.

Write down three things that get you fired up – it could be a pet peeve or problem you've encountered on your Pokémon journey.

1. _____

2. _____

3. _____

Now write down three things that light up your life – it could be your favourite Pokémon or your best friend.

1. _____

2. _____

3. _____

SING LOUD

Using the words below to inspire you, write a song about one of your great adventures or exciting memories.

ADVENTURE

FUN

POKÉMON

HAPPY

AWESOME

_____

_____

_____

_____

_____

_____

_____

_____

_____

_____

**Make up a dance to go
along with your new song.
Now perform the song
and dance for your family,
friends or Pokémon!**

_____

_____

THINK FAST

Write down all your answers about your favourite things as lightning-fast as you can below. The quicker you do it, the more likely your answers are going to be honest and accurate. You might even surprise yourself with what you put!

My favourite...

Book: _____

Animal: _____

Sport: _____

Pokémon: _____

Film: _____

Country: _____

Outfit: _____

Game: _____

Colour: _____

Shop: _____

Band: _____

Day: _____

Draw and colour Pikachu in the grid below.
Try copying the picture section by section.

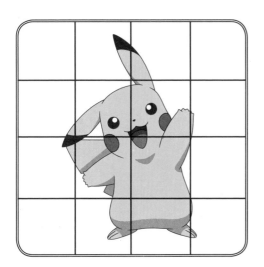

Those little round cheeks – while being cute and puffy – are full of electricity so beware of getting zapped!

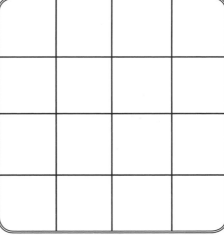

TIME TO EVOLVE

When Pokémon evolve, they get bigger and stronger, and they gain new skills.

What's a skill or strength you have that could be even stronger?

_____

_____

_____

What do you need to work on so that you could evolve into a stronger version of yourself? You can always ask your family and friends to help you!

_____

_____

_____

As you discover more Pokémon, your opinion can change. Answer these questions and look back on them. Which Pokémon do you think is...

the funniest? _____

the coolest? _____

the silliest? _____

SLEEPING SECRETS

When you're sleeping soundly like a Snorlax, have you ever wondered what your dreams mean? Read on to discover what your dreams say about you...

Water

Water in dreams can represent your emotions, so the type of water is important! A waterfall might mean that you should go with the flow, and a stormy sea could show that you're feeling a bit unsettled.

Flying

If you were dreaming of soaring high in the sky, then you must be flying high on life. Whether you achieved a goal or aced a test in school, you're feeling empowered and floating on cloud nine.

Being Chased

If you're being chased in your dream, it might mean that you're running away from something or someone in real life. Is there anything you're worried about? Talking to a friend or an adult you trust will help you feel less anxious.

Capture your dreams! The dreams you have when you're asleep can have surprising and powerful meanings. Record a whole week of your dreams here.

Monday

Tuesday

Wednesday

Thursday

Friday

Saturday

Sunday

SUPER SPOOKY

Some Pokémon are just ghastly and can give you nightmares.

Which Pokémon are you most frightened of? Why?

Design a new Ghost-type Pokémon to scare your friends.

Name: _____

What powers does it have?

_____

_____

FUTURE FUN

Pokémon can be unpredictable. Where do you think you and your friends will be ten years from now? Write down your predictions here so you can see how many come true.

Me

I will live in: _____ **With:** _____

My job will be: _____

My Friend

Name: _____ **They will live in:** _____

Their job will be: _____

Keep this page and look back at it with your friends to see how far you've gone on your Pokémon journey!

My Friend

Name: _____ **They will live in:** _____

Their job will be: _____

My Friend

Name: _____ **They will live in:** _____

Their job will be: _____

Most likely to...

travel to all the Pokémon regions: _____

catch 'em all: _____

become a Gym Leader: _____

design a new invention: _____

STAY GROUNDED

It's time to dig a little deeper into your feelings!

What makes me feel better when I'm having a bad day:

_____

_____

What I do when I'm in a good mood:

_____

_____

What makes my Pokémon feel better when they are having a bad day:

_____

_____

What makes you feel...

more stressed than Psyduck:

_____

angrier than Charizard:

_____

happier than Eevee:

_____

**sleepier than
a Snorlax:**

_____

POKÉMON PUNS

Pokémon love to have fun!

Write about one of the funniest moments you've had with your Pokémon:

Draw a picture of your favourite Pokémon pulling a silly face.

**Here are some of the best Pokémon puns out there –
you got to hear 'em all!**

Q: What appears over Ash's head when he gets an idea?
A: A lightbulbasaur!

Q: Why did the Squirtle cross the ocean?
A: To get to the other tide!

Q: What do you call Meowth's reflection?
A: copycat.

Q: How do you get Pikachu on a bus?
A: Poke him on.

Now try writing your own Pokémon jokes and puns here.

TIME TO PARTY

You work hard and train hard with your Pokémon so it's important to have fun together. Plan an awesome party with your Pokémon and celebrate how amazing you are.

Cook up a storm, just like Mallow. What snacks will you have at your party?

_____

_____

Pick your playlist to get everyone up and dancing like Ludicolo!

Song: _____ **Artist:** _____

What other entertainment will you have at your party?

_____

Create your party invitation here!

I choose you!

Catch all the fun at _____ **party!**

Date: _____

Time: _____

Place: _____

RSVP: _____

It's time for some quick-fire questions!
Would you rather catch...

a Scorbunny
or a Gyarados?
Why?

a Wooloo or a
Mimikyu?
Why?

a Pikachu or a
Zamazenta?
Why?

a Snorlax or a
Psyduck?
Why?

a Grookey or
an Alcremie?
Why?

SUPER SNAPSHOTS

You've shared some amazing adventures with your Pokémon, and there's more to come! Use this space to make a collage using your favourite Pokémon photos or drawings.

DREAM BIG

Dreaming big is amazing, but little dreams are at the heart of every great achievement. Turn your year into twelve mini adventures by setting yourself a goal for each month.

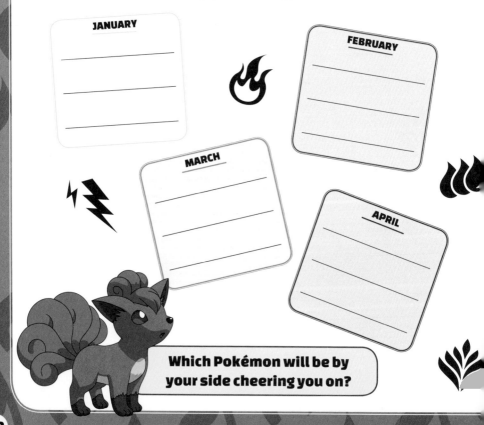

JANUARY

FEBRUARY

MARCH

APRIL

Which Pokémon will be by your side cheering you on?

MAY

JUNE

AUGUST

JULY

SEPTEMBER

OCTOBER

NOVEMBER

DECEMBER

GO GET 'EM

You've started on an exciting journey to become a true Trainer and the adventure is just beginning! Set yourself five goals and see if you can achieve them this year — think about what you want to achieve as a Pokémon Trainer.

1.

_____

_____

_____

2.

_____

_____